THIS WORK PLANNER

Belongs To:

_____

Nobody Cares, Work Harder

My Monthly WORK PLANNER

MONTH OF:

MOST IMPORTANT TASKS

MONDAY	TUESDAY	WEDNESDAY	THURSDAY	FRIDAY	SATURDAY	SUNDAY

NOTES

Weekly WORK PLANNER

MONDAY

TUESDAY

WEDNESDAY

THURSDAY

FRIDAY

SATURDAY

SUNDAY

WEEK OF

TOP PRIORITIES

DEADLINES	DUE ON

TO-DO LIST

APPOINTMENTS

MEETINGS

REMINDERS

NOTES

NOTES

Weekly WORK PLANNER

MONDAY

WEEK OF

TOP PRIORITIES

TUESDAY

DEADLINES	DUE ON

WEDNESDAY

THURSDAY

TO-DO LIST

FRIDAY

SATURDAY

SUNDAY

APPOINTMENTS

MEETINGS

REMINDERS

NOTES

NOTES

Weekly WORK PLANNER

MONDAY

TUESDAY

WEDNESDAY

THURSDAY

FRIDAY

SATURDAY

SUNDAY

WEEK OF

TOP PRIORITIES

DEADLINES	DUE ON

TO-DO LIST

APPOINTMENTS

MEETINGS

REMINDERS

NOTES

NOTES

Weekly WORK PLANNER

MONDAY

WEEK OF

TOP PRIORITIES

TUESDAY

| DEADLINES | DUE ON |

WEDNESDAY

THURSDAY

TO-DO LIST

FRIDAY

SATURDAY

SUNDAY

APPOINTMENTS

MEETINGS

REMINDERS

NOTES

NOTES

My Monthly WORK PLANNER

MONTH OF:

MOST IMPORTANT TASKS

- ○
- ○
- ○
- ○
- ○
- ○

MONDAY	TUESDAY	WEDNESDAY	THURSDAY	FRIDAY	SATURDAY	SUNDAY

NOTES

Weekly WORK PLANNER

MONDAY

WEEK OF

TUESDAY

TOP PRIORITIES

WEDNESDAY

DEADLINES	DUE ON

THURSDAY

TO-DO LIST

FRIDAY

SATURDAY

SUNDAY

APPOINTMENTS

MEETINGS

REMINDERS

NOTES

NOTES

Weekly WORK PLANNER

MONDAY

TUESDAY

WEDNESDAY

THURSDAY

FRIDAY

SATURDAY

SUNDAY

WEEK OF

TOP PRIORITIES

DEADLINES	DUE ON

TO-DO LIST

APPOINTMENTS

MEETINGS

REMINDERS

NOTES

NOTES

Weekly WORK PLANNER

MONDAY

WEEK OF

TOP PRIORITIES

TUESDAY

DEADLINES	DUE ON

WEDNESDAY

THURSDAY

TO-DO LIST

FRIDAY

SATURDAY

SUNDAY

APPOINTMENTS

MEETINGS

REMINDERS

NOTES

NOTES

Weekly WORK PLANNER

MONDAY

TUESDAY

WEDNESDAY

THURSDAY

FRIDAY

SATURDAY

SUNDAY

WEEK OF

TOP PRIORITIES

DEADLINES	DUE ON

TO-DO LIST

APPOINTMENTS

MEETINGS

REMINDERS

NOTES

NOTES

My Monthly **WORK PLANNER**

MONTH OF:

MOST IMPORTANT TASKS

MONDAY	TUESDAY	WEDNESDAY	THURSDAY	FRIDAY	SATURDAY	SUNDAY

NOTES

Weekly WORK PLANNER

MONDAY

TUESDAY

WEDNESDAY

THURSDAY

FRIDAY

SATURDAY

SUNDAY

WEEK OF

TOP PRIORITIES

DEADLINES | **DUE ON**

TO-DO LIST

APPOINTMENTS

MEETINGS

REMINDERS

NOTES

NOTES

Weekly WORK PLANNER

MONDAY

WEEK OF

TOP PRIORITIES

TUESDAY

DEADLINES	DUE ON

WEDNESDAY

THURSDAY

TO-DO LIST

FRIDAY

SATURDAY

SUNDAY

APPOINTMENTS

REMINDERS

MEETINGS

NOTES

NOTES

Weekly WORK PLANNER

MONDAY

TUESDAY

WEDNESDAY

THURSDAY

FRIDAY

SATURDAY

SUNDAY

WEEK OF

TOP PRIORITIES

DEADLINES	DUE ON

TO-DO LIST

APPOINTMENTS

MEETINGS

REMINDERS

NOTES

NOTES

Weekly WORK PLANNER

MONDAY

WEEK OF

TOP PRIORITIES

TUESDAY

DEADLINES | **DUE ON**

WEDNESDAY

THURSDAY

TO-DO LIST

FRIDAY

SATURDAY

SUNDAY

APPOINTMENTS

MEETINGS

REMINDERS

NOTES

NOTES

My Monthly WORK PLANNER

MONTH OF:

MOST IMPORTANT TASKS

MONDAY	TUESDAY	WEDNESDAY	THURSDAY	FRIDAY	SATURDAY	SUNDAY

NOTES

Weekly WORK PLANNER

MONDAY

WEEK OF

TOP PRIORITIES

TUESDAY

| DEADLINES | DUE ON |

WEDNESDAY

THURSDAY

TO-DO LIST

FRIDAY

SATURDAY

SUNDAY

APPOINTMENTS

MEETINGS

REMINDERS

NOTES

NOTES

Weekly WORK PLANNER

MONDAY

WEEK OF

TUESDAY

TOP PRIORITIES

WEDNESDAY

DEADLINES | **DUE ON**

THURSDAY

TO-DO LIST

FRIDAY

SATURDAY

SUNDAY

APPOINTMENTS

MEETINGS

REMINDERS

NOTES

NOTES

Weekly WORK PLANNER

MONDAY

WEEK OF

TUESDAY

TOP PRIORITIES

WEDNESDAY

DEADLINES	DUE ON

THURSDAY

TO-DO LIST

FRIDAY

SATURDAY

SUNDAY

APPOINTMENTS

MEETINGS

REMINDERS

NOTES

NOTES

Weekly WORK PLANNER

MONDAY

TUESDAY

WEDNESDAY

THURSDAY

FRIDAY

SATURDAY

SUNDAY

WEEK OF

TOP PRIORITIES

DEADLINES	DUE ON

TO-DO LIST

APPOINTMENTS

MEETINGS

REMINDERS

NOTES

NOTES

My Monthly WORK PLANNER

MONTH OF:

MOST IMPORTANT TASKS

MONDAY   TUESDAY   WEDNESDAY   THURSDAY   FRIDAY   SATURDAY   SUNDAY

NOTES

Weekly WORK PLANNER

MONDAY

TUESDAY

WEDNESDAY

THURSDAY

FRIDAY

SATURDAY

SUNDAY

WEEK OF

TOP PRIORITIES

DEADLINES | **DUE ON**

TO-DO LIST

APPOINTMENTS

MEETINGS

REMINDERS

NOTES

NOTES

Weekly WORK PLANNER

MONDAY

WEEK OF

TOP PRIORITIES

TUESDAY

DEADLINES | **DUE ON**

WEDNESDAY

THURSDAY

TO-DO LIST

FRIDAY

SATURDAY

SUNDAY

APPOINTMENTS

MEETINGS

REMINDERS

NOTES

NOTES

Weekly WORK PLANNER

MONDAY

TUESDAY

WEDNESDAY

THURSDAY

FRIDAY

SATURDAY

SUNDAY

WEEK OF

TOP PRIORITIES

DEADLINES	**DUE ON**

TO-DO LIST

APPOINTMENTS

MEETINGS

REMINDERS

NOTES

NOTES

Weekly WORK PLANNER

MONDAY

WEEK OF

TUESDAY

TOP PRIORITIES

WEDNESDAY

DEADLINES | DUE ON

THURSDAY

TO-DO LIST

FRIDAY

SATURDAY

SUNDAY

APPOINTMENTS

MEETINGS

REMINDERS

NOTES

NOTES

My Monthly **WORK PLANNER**

MONTH OF:

MOST IMPORTANT TASKS

MONDAY	TUESDAY	WEDNESDAY	THURSDAY	FRIDAY	SATURDAY	SUNDAY

NOTES

Weekly WORK PLANNER

MONDAY

WEEK OF

TOP PRIORITIES

TUESDAY

DEADLINES	DUE ON

WEDNESDAY

THURSDAY

TO-DO LIST

FRIDAY

SATURDAY

SUNDAY

APPOINTMENTS

MEETINGS

REMINDERS

NOTES

NOTES

Weekly WORK PLANNER

MONDAY

TUESDAY

WEDNESDAY

THURSDAY

FRIDAY

SATURDAY

SUNDAY

WEEK OF

TOP PRIORITIES

DEADLINES | **DUE ON**

TO-DO LIST

APPOINTMENTS

MEETINGS

REMINDERS

NOTES

NOTES

Weekly WORK PLANNER

MONDAY

WEEK OF

TUESDAY

TOP PRIORITIES

WEDNESDAY

DEADLINES	DUE ON

THURSDAY

TO-DO LIST

FRIDAY

SATURDAY

SUNDAY

APPOINTMENTS

MEETINGS

REMINDERS

NOTES

NOTES

Weekly WORK PLANNER

MONDAY

TUESDAY

WEDNESDAY

THURSDAY

FRIDAY

SATURDAY

SUNDAY

WEEK OF

TOP PRIORITIES

DEADLINES	**DUE ON**

TO-DO LIST

APPOINTMENTS

MEETINGS

REMINDERS

NOTES

NOTES

My Monthly **WORK PLANNER**

MONTH OF:

MOST IMPORTANT TASKS

MONDAY	TUESDAY	WEDNESDAY	THURSDAY	FRIDAY	SATURDAY	SUNDAY

NOTES

Weekly WORK PLANNER

MONDAY

WEEK OF

TUESDAY

TOP PRIORITIES

WEDNESDAY

DEADLINES | **DUE ON**

THURSDAY

TO-DO LIST

FRIDAY

SATURDAY

SUNDAY

APPOINTMENTS

MEETINGS

REMINDERS

NOTES

NOTES

Weekly WORK PLANNER

MONDAY

WEEK OF

TUESDAY

TOP PRIORITIES

DEADLINES	DUE ON

WEDNESDAY

THURSDAY

TO-DO LIST

FRIDAY

SATURDAY

SUNDAY

APPOINTMENTS

MEETINGS

REMINDERS

NOTES

NOTES

Weekly WORK PLANNER

MONDAY

TUESDAY

WEDNESDAY

THURSDAY

FRIDAY

SATURDAY

SUNDAY

WEEK OF

TOP PRIORITIES

DEADLINES	DUE ON

TO-DO LIST

APPOINTMENTS

MEETINGS

REMINDERS

NOTES

NOTES

Weekly WORK PLANNER

MONDAY

WEEK OF

TUESDAY

TOP PRIORITIES

WEDNESDAY

DEADLINES	DUE ON

THURSDAY

TO-DO LIST

FRIDAY

SATURDAY

SUNDAY

APPOINTMENTS

MEETINGS

REMINDERS

NOTES

NOTES

My Monthly **WORK PLANNER**

MONTH OF:

MOST IMPORTANT TASKS

MONDAY	TUESDAY	WEDNESDAY	THURSDAY	FRIDAY	SATURDAY	SUNDAY

NOTES

Weekly WORK PLANNER

MONDAY

WEEK OF

TUESDAY

TOP PRIORITIES

WEDNESDAY

DEADLINES	DUE ON

THURSDAY

TO-DO LIST

FRIDAY

SATURDAY

SUNDAY

APPOINTMENTS

MEETINGS

REMINDERS

NOTES

NOTES

Weekly WORK PLANNER

MONDAY

TUESDAY

WEDNESDAY

THURSDAY

FRIDAY

SATURDAY

SUNDAY

WEEK OF

TOP PRIORITIES

DEADLINES	DUE ON

TO-DO LIST

APPOINTMENTS

MEETINGS

REMINDERS

NOTES

NOTES

Weekly WORK PLANNER

MONDAY

WEEK OF

TUESDAY

TOP PRIORITIES

WEDNESDAY

DEADLINES	DUE ON

THURSDAY

TO-DO LIST

FRIDAY

SATURDAY

SUNDAY

APPOINTMENTS

MEETINGS

REMINDERS

NOTES

NOTES

Weekly WORK PLANNER

MONDAY

TUESDAY

WEDNESDAY

THURSDAY

FRIDAY

SATURDAY

SUNDAY

WEEK OF

TOP PRIORITIES

DEADLINES | **DUE ON**

TO-DO LIST

APPOINTMENTS

MEETINGS

REMINDERS

NOTES

NOTES

My Monthly **WORK PLANNER**

MONTH OF:

MOST IMPORTANT TASKS

MONDAY	TUESDAY	WEDNESDAY	THURSDAY	FRIDAY	SATURDAY	SUNDAY

NOTES

Weekly WORK PLANNER

MONDAY

TUESDAY

WEDNESDAY

THURSDAY

FRIDAY

SATURDAY

SUNDAY

WEEK OF

TOP PRIORITIES

DEADLINES | **DUE ON**

TO-DO LIST

APPOINTMENTS

MEETINGS

REMINDERS

NOTES

NOTES

Weekly WORK PLANNER

MONDAY

WEEK OF

TUESDAY

TOP PRIORITIES

WEDNESDAY

DEADLINES	DUE ON

THURSDAY

TO-DO LIST

FRIDAY

SATURDAY

SUNDAY

APPOINTMENTS

MEETINGS

REMINDERS

NOTES

NOTES

Weekly WORK PLANNER

MONDAY

TUESDAY

WEDNESDAY

THURSDAY

FRIDAY

SATURDAY

SUNDAY

WEEK OF

TOP PRIORITIES

DEADLINES	DUE ON

TO-DO LIST

APPOINTMENTS

MEETINGS

REMINDERS

NOTES

NOTES

Weekly WORK PLANNER

MONDAY

WEEK OF

TUESDAY

TOP PRIORITIES

WEDNESDAY

DEADLINES	DUE ON

THURSDAY

FRIDAY

TO-DO LIST

SATURDAY

SUNDAY

APPOINTMENTS

MEETINGS

REMINDERS

NOTES

NOTES

My Monthly **WORK PLANNER**

MONTH OF:

MOST IMPORTANT TASKS

MONDAY	TUESDAY	WEDNESDAY	THURSDAY	FRIDAY	SATURDAY	SUNDAY

NOTES

Weekly WORK PLANNER

MONDAY

WEEK OF

TUESDAY

TOP PRIORITIES

WEDNESDAY

DEADLINES	DUE ON

THURSDAY

TO-DO LIST

FRIDAY

SATURDAY

SUNDAY

APPOINTMENTS

MEETINGS

REMINDERS

NOTES

NOTES

Weekly WORK PLANNER

MONDAY

TUESDAY

WEDNESDAY

THURSDAY

FRIDAY

SATURDAY

SUNDAY

WEEK OF

TOP PRIORITIES

DEADLINES | **DUE ON**

TO-DO LIST

APPOINTMENTS

MEETINGS

REMINDERS

NOTES

NOTES

Weekly WORK PLANNER

MONDAY

WEEK OF

TUESDAY

TOP PRIORITIES

WEDNESDAY

DEADLINES	DUE ON

THURSDAY

TO-DO LIST

FRIDAY

SATURDAY

SUNDAY

APPOINTMENTS

MEETINGS

REMINDERS

NOTES

NOTES

Weekly WORK PLANNER

MONDAY

TUESDAY

WEDNESDAY

THURSDAY

FRIDAY

SATURDAY

SUNDAY

WEEK OF

TOP PRIORITIES

DEADLINES	DUE ON

TO-DO LIST

APPOINTMENTS

MEETINGS

REMINDERS

NOTES

NOTES

My Monthly **WORK PLANNER**

MONTH OF:

MOST IMPORTANT TASKS

MONDAY	TUESDAY	WEDNESDAY	THURSDAY	FRIDAY	SATURDAY	SUNDAY

NOTES

Weekly WORK PLANNER

MONDAY

TUESDAY

WEDNESDAY

THURSDAY

FRIDAY

SATURDAY

SUNDAY

WEEK OF

TOP PRIORITIES

DEADLINES	DUE ON

TO-DO LIST

APPOINTMENTS

MEETINGS

REMINDERS

NOTES

NOTES

Weekly WORK PLANNER

MONDAY

WEEK OF

TOP PRIORITIES

TUESDAY

DEADLINES   **DUE ON**

WEDNESDAY

THURSDAY

TO-DO LIST

FRIDAY

SATURDAY

SUNDAY

APPOINTMENTS

MEETINGS

REMINDERS

NOTES

NOTES

Weekly WORK PLANNER

MONDAY

TUESDAY

WEDNESDAY

THURSDAY

FRIDAY

SATURDAY

SUNDAY

WEEK OF

TOP PRIORITIES

DEADLINES	DUE ON

TO-DO LIST

APPOINTMENTS

MEETINGS

REMINDERS

NOTES

NOTES

Weekly WORK PLANNER

MONDAY

WEEK OF

TOP PRIORITIES

TUESDAY

DEADLINES	DUE ON

WEDNESDAY

THURSDAY

TO-DO LIST

FRIDAY

SATURDAY

SUNDAY

APPOINTMENTS

MEETINGS

REMINDERS

NOTES

NOTES

My Monthly WORK PLANNER

MONTH OF:

MOST IMPORTANT TASKS

MONDAY	TUESDAY	WEDNESDAY	THURSDAY	FRIDAY	SATURDAY	SUNDAY

NOTES

Weekly WORK PLANNER

MONDAY

WEEK OF

TOP PRIORITIES

TUESDAY

DEADLINES	DUE ON

WEDNESDAY

THURSDAY

TO-DO LIST

FRIDAY

SATURDAY

SUNDAY

APPOINTMENTS

MEETINGS

REMINDERS

NOTES

NOTES

Weekly WORK PLANNER

MONDAY

TUESDAY

WEDNESDAY

THURSDAY

FRIDAY

SATURDAY

SUNDAY

WEEK OF

TOP PRIORITIES

DEADLINES	DUE ON

TO-DO LIST

APPOINTMENTS

MEETINGS

REMINDERS

NOTES

NOTES

Weekly WORK PLANNER

MONDAY

WEEK OF

TUESDAY

TOP PRIORITIES

WEDNESDAY

DEADLINES	DUE ON

THURSDAY

TO-DO LIST

FRIDAY

SATURDAY

SUNDAY

APPOINTMENTS

MEETINGS

REMINDERS

NOTES

NOTES

Weekly WORK PLANNER

MONDAY

TUESDAY

WEDNESDAY

THURSDAY

FRIDAY

SATURDAY

SUNDAY

WEEK OF

TOP PRIORITIES

DEADLINES | **DUE ON**

TO-DO LIST

APPOINTMENTS

MEETINGS

REMINDERS

NOTES

NOTES

Made in the USA
Middletown, DE
27 November 2019